THANKSGIVING

This book belongs to

_____

Knock Knock!
Who's there?
Iran!
Iran who?
Iran over here to get some stuffing!

Knock Knock!
Who's there?
Whadoo!
Whadoo who?
Whadoo you think is for dessert?

Knock Knock!
Who's there?
Jacklyn.
Jacklyn who?
Jacklyn Hyde!

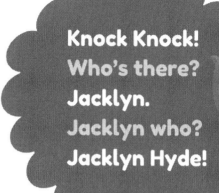

Knock Knock!
Who's there?
Essen!
Essen who?
Essen it fun to
listen to these
Thanksgiving jokes!

Knock Knock!
Who's there?
Ivan.
Ivan who?
Ivan to eat some turkey!

Knock Knock!
Who's there?
Phillip.
Phillip who?
Phillip my bag with treats!

Knock Knock!
Who's there?
Frank.
Frank who?
Frankenstein!

Knock Knock!
Who's there?
Gladys
Gladys Who?
Gladys Thanksgiving.
Aren't you?

Knock Knock!
Who's there?
Olive.
Olive who?
Olive Thanksgiving!

Knock Knock!
Who's there?
Tank!
Tank who?
Tankful for this amazing dinner!

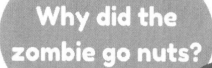

Why did the zombie go nuts?

He lost his mind!

Knock Knock!
Who's there?
Harry.
Harry who?
Harry up I'm starving!

Why didn't the zombie get the role in the movie?

The director wanted someone livelier!

Why did the zombie comedian get Booed off stage?

Because all his jokes were rotten!

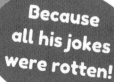

What kind of vehicle do zombies drive?

Monster trucks

What did the zombie say after eating the comedian?

This tastes funny!

What's a baby zombie's favorite toy?

A deady bear

What candy do ghouls hate the most?

Life Savers

Where do zombies go on vacation?

To the Deaditerranean!

Who won the zombie race?

Nobody. It was DEAD even!

What does a zombie get when he's late for a date?

The cold shoulder

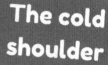

How are zombies like computers?

They both have megabites!

Why did the zombie quit his teaching job?

Because he only had 1 pupil left!

Who do cowboy zombies fight?

The Deadskins

Why can't skeleton musicians perform at church?

Because they have no organs!

What does it take to become a vampire?

Deadication

What do monkey ghosts like to eat?

Boonanas

What sport do vampires like the most?

Batminton

Why did the apple pie start crying?

Because its peelings were hurt.

What happened to the witch with the upside-down nose?

Her hat blew off every time she sneezed!

Which monster is round, red and doesn't come out till autumn ends?

Applestein

Who helps the kid pumpkins cross the street at school?

The crossing gourd

How do you talk in the apple library?

By using your incider voice!

What monster is round, red and comes out during fall?

Frankenapple

Why do trees lose their leaves in the fall?

I don't know, it's just autumn-matic!

What type of trees do ghosts love?

Ceme-trees

How does an elephant get down from a tree?

It sits on a leaf and waits till fall.

What happens when winter comes?

Autumn leaves.

Why do leaves change color in autumn?

Because they chloro-empty instead of chlorophyll.

What do you call a pepper in late autumn?

A little chilli

What is a tree's least favorite month of the year?

Septimber

Why does Humpty Dumpty hate autumn?

Because that's when he has a great fall.

What did the tree say at the end of the argument with fall?

That's it. I'm leafing!

What condition causes you to believe that fall isn't here?

Disbe-leaf

How is the tree doing now that it's autumn?

He had to take paid leaf.

How do leaves get from place to place?

With autumn-mobiles

How do you fix a broken pumpkin?

With a pumpkin patch.

What is the cutest season?

Awwtumn

What did the tree say to autumn?

Leaf me alone!

What did one autumn leaf say to the other?

I'm falling for you.

What happened to the Pilgrim who was shot by a bow?

He had an arrow escape!

Why didn't the Pilgrims tell secrets in the corn field?

Because the corn had ears.

Where do turkeys go to dance?

The Butterball

What did the hipster say the morning after Thanksgiving?

I liked the turkey before it was cool.

Why did the handbag catch a ride with the Pilgrims?

To avoid purse-cution.

What's your favorite Thanksgiving food?

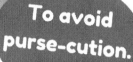

I know it's irrational but it's pi.

How many cooks does it take to stuff a turkey?

Just one but you have to really squeeze them in.

Why was the cook late to Thanksgiving dinner?

He lost track of thyme!

What does a Pilgrim call his friends?

Pal-grims

What can you never eat for Thanksgiving dinner?

Breakfast and lunch

How many cranberries grow on a bush?

All of them.

What kind of car does a Pilgrim drive?

A Plymouth

Why did the Pilgrims sail?

Because they missed their flight!

When the Pilgrims finally landed, where did they stand?

On their feet.

If the Pilgrims were alive today, what would they be most famous for?

Their age

What smells the most at a Thanksgiving dinner?

Your nose

Why did the turkey want to see the movie so badly?

Because it had Gregory Peck in it.

What did the mom say to her son when he asked for a pet parrot for Thanksgiving?

No you'll be having turkey like everyone else.

What's the best dance to do on Thanksgiving?

The turkey trot.

What does a turkey like to eat on Thanksgiving?

Nothing – it's already stuffed.

What sound does a turkey's phone make?

Wing wing

What's a Pilgrim's grandma called?

Pilgranny

How do you get a turkey to fly internationally?

By getting a bird class ticket.

What do you get when you cross a turkey and a banjo?

A turkey that can pluck itself.

What's a pumpkin's favorite sport?

Squash

What do Halloween and Thanksgiving have in common?

One has goblins and the other has gobblers!

What happens when a turkey lays an egg on a hill?

An eggroll

Why did the bubble gum cross the road?

It was stuck on the turkey's foot.

What showed how much the Mayflower liked America?

The way it hugged the shore.

What did the boy say when his Mom wanted help to fix Thanksgiving dinner?

But I didn't break it!

How are a turkey, monkey and donkey all alike?

They all carry keys on them.

What do turkeys like to have on nice and sunny days?

Pecknics

What do you call a turkey fumbling the ball in football?

A fowl play

When is turkey soup bad for you health?

When you're the turkey!

What did the turkey say to the turkey hunter?

Quack, quack

When does Christmas come before Thanksgiving?

In the dictionary.

What do you get when you cross a Pilgrim with a cracker?

A Pilgraham

Why did the Pilgrim's pants keep falling down?

Because his belt was on his hat.

Why do turkeys lay eggs?

Because if they dropped them, they would break!

Can a turkey jump higher than the Empire State Building?

Of course! Buildings can't jump.

What do you call the spirit that takes away Pilgrims at night?

The Pilgrim Reaper

What's the most musical part of a turkey?

The drumstick

What do you call the feathers on a turkey?

Turkey feathers

What's the best thing to put into a pumpkin pie?

Your teeth

What unit of measurement is the smallest for a Pilgrim?

Pilgram

What do turkeys on space stations say?

Hubble, hubble

Why did the turkey cross the road twice?

To show he wasn't chicken!

What always comes at the end of Thanksgiving?

The letter G

Why was the Thanksgiving dinner so expensive?

It had 24 carrots.

What do you call raining turkeys?

Fowl weather

What did the Mayflower sailors play when they were bored?

Cards - since they always have a deck.

If fruit comes from a fruit tree, where does turkey come from?

A poul-tree

Where did the first corn come from?

The stalk brought it.

If April showers bring in May flowers, what do May flowers bring?

Pilgrims

What do Pilgrims learn in school?

Pilgrammar

What is a scarecrow's favorite fruit?

Straw-berries

What kind of face do Pilgrims make when in pain?

Pilgrimace

What do comedians call Thanksgiving?

Pranksgiving

Why did the turkey cross the road?

To get to the other side.

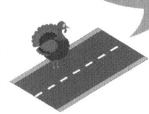

What do you call Thanksgiving for selfish people?

Thankstaking

How were clothes cleaned on the Mayflower?

Tide

How did the scarecrow win the Nobel Prize?

By being outstanding in his field!

What kind of music did the Pilgrims used to listen to?

Plymouth rock

What do you use to make Thanksgiving bread?

May flour

How did the Pilgrims bring their cows to America?

On the Mooooo-flower!

What's the cross between a turkey and a ghost?

A poultrygeis

Where did they take the Mayflower when it was sick?

The nearest doc

How did Mayflower sailors say hello to one another?

They waved.

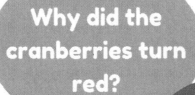

What do you get when you cross a turkey with a centipede?

Drumsticks for everyone on Thanksgiving!

What did the turkey say to the PC?

Google, google

What sound does a limping turkey make?

Wobble, wobble

What did one turkey say to the other when it saw the Pilgrims land at Plymouth rock?

They seem nice. Maybe they'll have us over for dinner!

Why do turkeys always go "gobble gobble"?

Because they never learned good manners.

Why did Billy get low grades after Thanksgiving?

Because everything gets marked down during the holidays.

What kind of bugs go oui oui buzz buzz on Thanksgiving?

French flies

What key has legs but can't open doors?

Turkeys

Why can you never take a turkey to church?

Because of their fowl language.

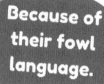

What's everyone's favorite vegetable on Thanksgiving?

Beets me.

What's the key to a great Thanksgiving dinner?

The turKEY

How can you make a turkey float?

You need 2 scoops of ice cream, root beer and some turkey!

What happened when the turkey got into a brawl?

He got the stuffing knocked out of him.

Why did the turkey cross the road?

Because it was the chicken's day off.

If Thanksgiving was taken off the calendar, what would you have left?

A week with only 6 days!

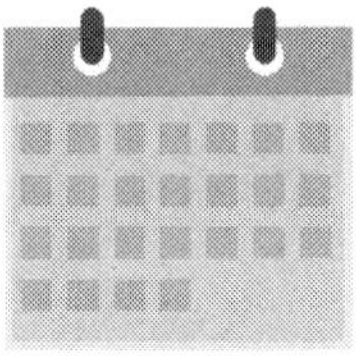

What is the ratio of a pumpkin's circumference to its diameter?

Pumpkin pi

When is the best time to eat turkey?

When it's cooked and on the dinner table.

Why did the boy come to school late the day after Thanksgiving?

Because it was Black Friday and he took 50% off the day.

Why do turkeys gobble?

Because they can't talk.

Who gets full the quickest on Thanksgiving?

The turkey because it's already stuffed!

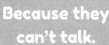

Why were turkeys parading down the street?

They were marching to the beat of their drumsticks.

If a turkey spent all night relaxing in fragrant oils, what would it be the next morning?

Marinated and ready for the oven!

Who is a turkey's favorite kind of person on Thanksgiving?

A vegetarian

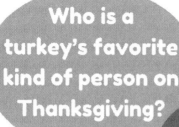

Why did the chicken cross the road?

Because the turkey ran away and he had to bring him back!

What did the turkey suggest for the families to eat on Thanksgiving?

Any food not fowl in smell or taste.

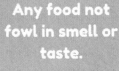

When do turkeys get nervous?

Because they see the calendars being flipped over to October/November!

Leave Your Feedback on Amazon

Please think about leaving some feedback via a review on Amazon. It may only take a moment, but it really does mean the world for small businesses like mine.

Even if you did not enjoy this title, please let us know the reason(s) in your review so that we may improve this title and serve you better.

From the Publisher

Hayden Fox's mission is to create premium content for children that will help them expand their vocabulary, grow their imaginations, gain confidence, and share tons of laughs along the way.

Without you, however, this would not be possible, so we sincerely thank you for your purchase and for supporting our company mission.

Made in the USA
Monee, IL
15 November 2022